Trains & Painted Moments

ADULT COLORING BOOK WITH POETRY AND SELF-DISCOVERY

Aventuras De Viaje

Copyright SF Nonfiction Books © 2024

All Rights Reserved

No part of this document may be reproduced without written consent from the author.

www.SFNonfictionBooks.com

INTRODUCTION

Welcome to a captivating world where the marvel of trains converges with the realm of creativity, where the timeless allure of these majestic machines meets the strokes of imagination. This is not merely a coloring book—it's a journey, a reflection, and a celebration of the inspiring beauty of trains and the painted moments they inspire.

Each page invites you to explore a realm filled with detailed illustrations of various trains and scenes, from the classic steam engines to modern locomotives, all awaiting your colors to bring them to life. These scenes, symbols of the world's rich railway heritage, call for your colors to reveal their stories. Coloring these moments offers not only a visual journey but also a profound connection with the majestic wonders of the railways.

In the hustle of our daily lives, finding moments to pause and appreciate the wonders of human ingenuity is invaluable. This book encourages you to slow down, immerse yourself in a world of intricate artistry and serene introspection, and reconnect with the timeless elegance of trains and creativity. It's an opportunity to reignite your imagination and infuse it with the colors of progress and self-discovery.

Begin this artistic journey, exploring the detailed realm of trains and the calming act of coloring. Here, you're not just witnessing the beauty of these magnificent machines; you're engaging with their wonders, unleashing your creativity, and experiencing the tranquility of artistic mindfulness.

Discovering the Mosaic of Imagination

Dive deeper, and you'll find that this book has been meticulously crafted to enhance your personal journey:

- **Simple Activities:** Beyond just coloring, engage with activities designed to spark reflection and creativity. These gentle prompts will lead you to moments of introspection, serving as kindling for your inner fire.

- **Quotes:** Let the wisdom of personal development accompany you, illuminating your path as you add your own burst of color to the pages.

- **Positive Affirmations:** As you color, let these words of positivity uplift your spirit, molding your thoughts and inspiring a brighter perspective.

- **Poems and Haikus:** Delight in the poetic tales that complement the theme of this book, capturing life's varied rhythms and experiences. Each verse and every line serve as a muse for your artistic endeavors, enhancing your coloring journey with lyrical inspiration.

Embark on this coloring odyssey, immersing yourself in a world of diverse themes and the therapeutic embrace of art. Each page invites you on a unique journey, blending your creativity with the tranquility of coloring.

THANKS FOR YOUR PURCHASE

Get Your Next SF Nonfiction Book FREE!

Claim the book of your choice at:

www.SFNonfictionBooks.com/Free-Book

You will also be among the first to know of all the latest releases, discount offers, bonus content, and more.

Go to:

www.SFNonfictionBooks.com/Free-Book

Thanks again for your support.

**Track Your Gratitude:
List three things that made you
feel grateful today.**

_____

_____

"Life is a journey, not a destination, and every track leads to self-discovery."
— *Ralph Waldo Emerson*

I am on the right track to achieving my goals.

The Journey's Call
On iron tracks we ride through time,
Past valleys deep and mountains high.
Each station brings a new found rhyme,
As onward, ever on, we fly.

Ticket to Kindness:
Describe a small act of kindness you performed or witnessed today.

_____

_____

"Every train ride teaches us something new about ourselves and the world around us."

I trust the process and embrace every stop along the way.

Morning Train
Dawn light on steel rails,
Whispers of a distant dream,
Tracks to new wonders.

Railway Moments:
What was a memorable moment from your day that brought you joy?

_____

_____

"A smooth track never made a skilled conductor."

I am moving forward with purpose and confidence.

Rails of Reflection

Through towns and fields, the engine roars,
A song of metal, steam, and fire.
With every mile, the spirit soars,
Inspired by this moving choir.

**Engine of Positivity:
Write about a positive thought
that powered your day.**

_____

_____

"In the rhythm of the rails, find the heartbeat of your own journey."

I find beauty in the experience, not just the destination.

Quiet Station
Stillness at the stop,
Life's stories wait to unfold,
Tracks gleam in moonlight.

Connections Made:
Describe a meaningful interaction you had with someone.

_____

_____

"Even the longest journeys begin with a single ticket."

I am patient and embrace each moment of my life.

The Conductor's Wisdom
He guides the train with steady hand,
Through stormy nights and sunny days.
His wisdom like the shifting sand,
Teaches us in subtle ways.

Path to Self-Discovery:
What did you learn about yourself this week?

_____

_____

"Like a train, life moves forward, and so must we."

I am open to new experiences and the growth they bring.

Passing Scenery

Fields of green and gold,
Flash by in a swift embrace,
Life's swift panorama.

Tracks of Time:
How did you spend a cherished moment recently?

_____

_____

"Trains remind us to stay on track, but also to enjoy the view."

I am grateful for the path and the lessons it brings.

Bridges to Horizons

Across the bridges, through the mist,
We travel forth to meet the dawn.
Each sunset gives the rails a kiss,
As night reveals another morn.

Railroad of Resilience:
Write about a challenge you overcame.

_____

_____

"The rails of life may be rigid, but our journey along them can be anything but."

I am in control of my life and embrace the unknown.

Rail Dreams

Rails hum a soft tune,
Dreams of far-off places call,
Night train journeys on.

Freight of Friendship:
How did a friend make your day better recently?

_____

_____

"In every journey, there is beauty, even in the stops and starts."

I am strong and capable of overcoming any obstacle on my track.

Echoes of the Past
Old steamers tell of days gone by,
Their whistles sing of history.
Beneath the ever-changing sky,
We find our own sweet mystery.

Engineer's Insight:
Write a reflection on a decision you made.

_____

_____

"In the rhythm of the rails, find peace and clarity."

I am connected to the rhythm of my path and find peace within it.

Endless Tracks

Tracks stretch to the sky,
Life's journey in parallel,
Boundless paths unfold.

**Tracks of Triumph:
Describe a personal victory you experienced.**

_____

_____

"The journey of a thousand miles begins with a single step—or a single train ride."
— *Adapted from Lao Tzu*

I find joy in every mile of my life.

Carriages of Thought

In carriages, we sit and dream,
Of futures bright and pasts recalled.
Our thoughts flow like a gentle stream,
As life's great mysteries are enthralled.

Station of Strength:
Write about a moment when you felt strong.

_____

_____

"Every stop along the journey is a chance to reflect and grow."

I am thankful for the progress I make each day.

Midnight Express
Stars guide through the dark,
Train whispers secrets of night,
Dreams ride on the wind.

Ticket to Tranquility:
How did you find a moment of tranquility recently?

_____

_____

"Embrace the journey, trust the process, and enjoy the ride."

BEYOND THESE PAGES

A Deeper Dive into Art and Soul Awaits!

This book is but a chapter in a voyage where creativity meets depth.

Craving more? Explore the link below and weave deeper into the tapestry of art and emotion.

www.SFNonfictionBooks.com/Adult-Coloring-Books

A HEARTFELT THANK YOU

Dear colorist,

Thank you for choosing this book. If you enjoyed your journey, please leave a review where you purchased it. Your feedback helps more than you might think.

As the colors on these pages come to life, so does our shared journey in this artistic realm. I am deeply grateful for your trust and for allowing this book to be part of your self-care and personal journey.

By coloring these pages, you've not just created art but also woven moments of peace, reflection, and creativity into your life.

If you wish to explore more, there are other themes awaiting your artistic touch. Dive into new worlds and let your imagination flow.

From the deepest corner of my heart, thank you for bringing this book to life. Until our next artistic adventure together, cherish the colors of your journey and continue to shine.

Warmly,

Aventuras De Viaje

ABOUT THE AUTHOR

Aventuras has three passions: travel, writing, and learning new skills.

Combining these three things, Miss Viaje spends her time exploring the world and learning about anything and everything that interests her, from yoga, to music, to science, and more.

Aventuras takes what she discovers and shares it through her books.

www.SFNonfictionBooks.com

www.ingramcontent.com/pod-product-compliance
Lightning Source LLC
Chambersburg PA
CBHW081621100526
44590CB00021B/3545